Color My Thoughts

Pamela J. Patterson; Rita J. Ray

authorHOUSE

AuthorHouse™
1663 Liberty Drive
Bloomington, IN 47403
www.authorhouse.com
Phone: 1 (800) 839-8640

Published by AuthorHouse   12/14/2016

ISBN: 978-1-5246-5435-1 (sc)
ISBN: 978-1-5246-5434-4 (e)

Library of Congress Control Number: 2016920558

Print information available on the last page.

Contents

I dedicate this book to the memory of Richard and Vergia Patterson, Henrietta Walker, Pauline Kynard and Wil Clay.

Pamela

I dedicate this book in memory of my sister Linda and my brother Tony. You live on in memories held in my heart.

Rita

Loving You

when I'm with you,
   my smile shames
      the sun;
   I'm happy, giddy,
childlike again,

like looking in a
   mirror, seeing a
      reflection
of someone
   not me,

     that girl is joyous,
her laughter flows
      freely loudly,

with a toss of hair
    and eyes brimming
   with Fourth of July
     sparkle,
she's obviously loved,
   desired,

am I her—
   finally?

I embrace you,
     and love you,
   and know that
you love me,

   sweeter than
a double-dip of
   chocolate curling
    down the sides of a
crisp sugar cone

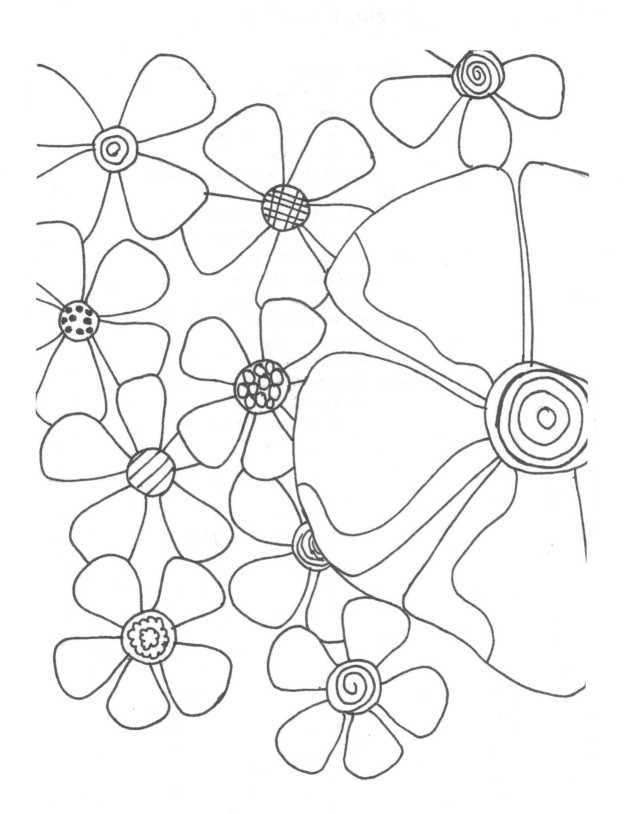

Night Thoughts

night thoughts seep
    into my consciousness,
      without warning or reason;
they pierce the empty darkness,
    invade the stillness
    and crouch beneath the moon's crawl;
night thoughts creep,
    as I sit curled upon my sofa,
      swaddled in cozy robe and slippers;
like old friends, they bring
    remembrance of times past,
      causing me to blush or weep;
night thoughts comfort me
    with familiar whispers of
      moments gone by;
sweet meditations that spiral
    through ghostly shadows,
      and wait for the tiptoe of dawn.

Can we take it slow?

as we travel love's terrain,
    can we please take it slow?
let's make this a Sunday stroll;

it's tempting,
   at the starting line,
to jump the gun, let the
    butterflies cause us to run;

   though the venture may
be thrilling, let's not accelerate
    out time, edge one another
out, seek happiness,
  but never pause to savor
the joy;

Yes, I realize,
   speed has its place,
    but, in our case,
victory will not come to the
   swift,
    but to the faithful;

So, please take my hand,
    meander with me along
  love's path, and let's
embrace a tepid pace

Praise

my days are overcast,
my bills are overdue,
my checkbook's overdrawn,
but, I'm gon' give some praise to you;

my blood pressure's shooting up,
and my cholesterol is, too,
I don't wanna get out of bed,
but, I gon' give some praise to you;

my kids are acting all crazy,
doing nothing they're s'posed to do,
Lord, they're getting on my nerves,
but, I gon' give some praise to you;

you've always been there for me,
you've always seen me through,
when nobody else could help me,
I knew I could turn to you,

So, I'm gon' lift my voice toward heaven
and I'm gon' give some praise to you!

Mementoes

Her 8x10 glossy, lovingly
framed in warm mahogany,
        sits atop
    your fireplace mantle,
overlooking grade-school
        snapshots
    of your children and
trophies that sprout baseball
    pitchers and twirling
        ballerinas; unlike the
woman who smiles so
    happily in the photo
        she's no longer
    in the home;
you say, she just up and left
    one day; you claim, you and
        the kids are better off
without her; but, like her
    smile, beaming among
        your fireplace mementoes,
her memory radiates your home;
        when you speak of her,
    with cautious glances
        toward the photo,
a softness in your eyes belies
    the acrid tone
        in your voice;
no one will ever replace
    the mistress of the hearth;
she'll remain forever nestled
        among the mementoes
    in your home and
        in your heart.

Poet

I write poems to unclothe hidden passions,
to expose falsely rendered misgivings, and

I write poems to expound unadulterated joy
in the midst of the agony of martyrdom, and

I write poems reflecting the grittiness of love,
while showcasing the arousal of despair, and

I write poems that allow calculated musings
to speak without rhyme, but with reason, and

I write poems of indistinct meter and inept
symmetry, and hope that you find beauty within

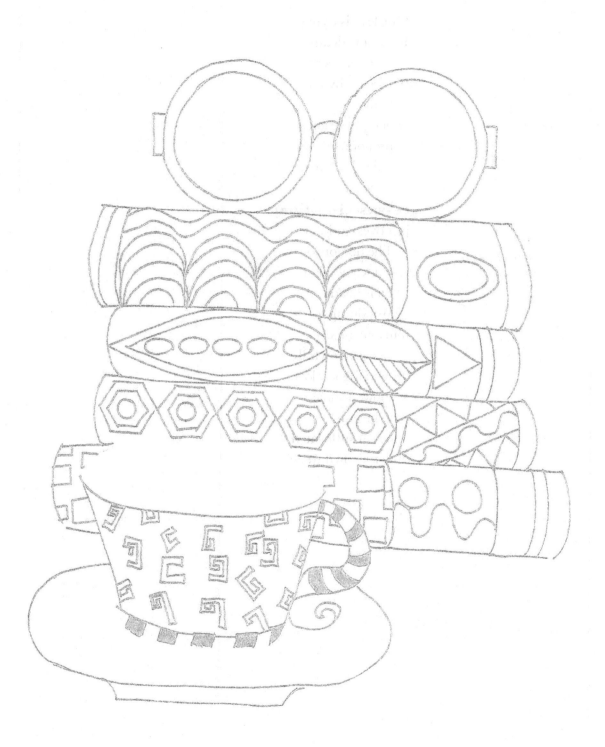

Breathing Room

Our love is dying.
It's a slow death,
   with vital signs
that cease by the
   hour;
When physicians
   pronounce
   it dead, there'll
   be no
re-sus-ci-ta-tion;
just over-and-out...
   The doctors of
   love will lower
   their heads
   and slump away,
murmuring ever
   so sorrowfully,
"It was a good love –
   showed some
     promise –
   but, it suffocated
under its own weight."

A Ribbon of Life

A ribbon forever binds us together;
    From a void of darkness it flowed,
a suture sealing wounds and giving
    meaning to misconceptions
and purpose to a lost being;

Pulsing with the breathes of God,
    whispering the sustenance of
a mother's love
    distant and unseen;

A ribbon stretched thin by birth,
    possessing strength of
generations past and desires
    yet hoped for;

No cut will truly sever or separate,
    for the ribbon swirls
between us, weaving a remembrance
    of heartbeats that spun with
an unborn sigh, and settled
    like dust along a
    well-worn path

Love...again

What do I write about today?
I've tired of writing about love,
coalescing rhymes –
          just rhetoric –
about something that defies
sanity or logic;

Many love poems have been
written because we don't
          understand the
               art of love;

We can't rationalize it or
formalize it, so we approach
     love with trepidation;

Like a belief in God, our
finite minds can't comprehend
His power, so we revere Him
          or we fear Him;

But, I don't want to write about
religion, for God is personal,
     and there's no confusion,
for only the fool says in his heart,
          there is no God;

Like the intimate conversing
of lovers, communing with God
          lays bare the
               incomprehensibility
               of true adoration,
which brings this poem back to love...
again

Yours Eternally

Let the last line of my ending poem be
a postscript of praise to you from me,
for when the rigors of this world are done,
I'll rest in peace 'cause I knew your Son;
so, with a broken heart and bended knee,
I vow to be only yours eternally

I've Known Moments

I've known moments of happiness –
    seconds, it seems;

  rollercoaster rides with family,
dancing till dawn with someone
called "the dancer,"

  glasses raised to the end of my
college days, my babies' smiles,
the luscious sounds of their
gurgled cooing;

I've known moments of sorrow –
    hours, it seems;

  lights twinkling on Christmas
eve – muted and silenced with
solitude,

  a heart breaking under a
wayward child, a hand held
as life slipped away,

  waking at midnight and
remembering the bitter taste
of a final kiss to someone once trusted.

On the Crest of a Storm

White-capped waves
  racing toward
    shore, expunged
    by hallows of
angry air;

while mouse-gray billows
  scamper across the
sky toward the end
    of day;

an impending wrath,
  exhaling gusts of wind
and melting the
    setting sun,

darkens the swelling
  body to a barbaric mass,
    threatening
everything
  in its wake;

the riled crests now
  cloaked in blackness,
rise and plunge furiously,
    ejecting skyward,
like a mountainous
  wall eclipsing the
horizon.

No Lies to Tell

There'll be no burden to unload,
  nothing to explain,
   no lies will unfold;

He's a good man, good as they come,
  while you're just a part-time lover,
looking for easy on the run;

Maybe, as they say, in another life,
  if you and I had met at another time,
perhaps, I'd be yours and not his wife;

But, for now, there's no justification,
  there's no reason for me to cheat,
so, there'll be no such validation;

With him, years will turn to gray;
  my eyes will close on this ol' world,
   and never look back and regret this day.

Old Lovers

I met an old lover on the street today,
    and wasn't quite sure what to do or say;
I quickly turned and took a breather,
    then realized he wasn't sure either;
We were both stiff and formal, how sad,
    considering all the fiery moments we'd had;
He and I feigned delight, as we came face to face,
    and patted the other's shoulder in an awkward embrace;
His once playful eyes, now shallow and bare,
    offered no trace of the passion once there;
The remembrance of our closeness caused me to blush,
    but not with an innocence that once made me gush;
I knew my feelings for him had long ago died,
    there was no sentiment I wanted to confide;
We'd obviously moved on, with new lovers each,
    with our pride intact and no secrets to breech;
Feeling relief, we simply smiled and walked away,
    just two, old lovers who passed on the street today.

Colors

your love colors
my mind with
iridescent
pastels; pale

as a distant
rainbow's
glow, steady as
the March winds
that blow;

crystal under the
sheen of a chilled
moon, lovers

out strolling
at midnight, truth
personified;

your love colors
my thoughts;
spraying a mist
of hue from the lips
of Cupid's own muse

More than a Sister

You had one husband, two kids,
and were a suburban housewife,
with a backyard flower garden
and a cozy, middle-class life;

I was the urban single mom,
with multiple careers,
and no-account love affairs,
juggling it all through years;

I shared everything with you,
knowing you'd always listen with love,
'cause no matter what I'd done,
it would never again be spoken of;

Sometimes, I'd smile as you would fuss
and fret your daily details,
knowing you'd object if I expressed
worry over my personal fails;

We painted beautiful rainbows
across miles and over the other's tears,
we sheltered one another's secrets,
and laughed away our fears

You were more than a sister,
you were my best friend,
a confidant and blessing that
only God could send

Irony

glutching this fading dream,
i'm searching for love's lost gleam,

ignoring the splitting seams
that expose all the lying schemes,

refusing to leave, so it seems,
my heart's riding a moonlit beam,

and while reality rudely screams,
my heart – love's defender –

dreams

Always

It's as if I've always
known you;
your thoughts –
reflections of my own;

Our smiles are frequent
and light, like summer clouds,
appearing simultaneously,
without foresight or
sentiment;

Our hearts beat a
rhythmic history,
co-joined in the
garden; forbidden
before time; so
familiar;

We emerge from
different backgrounds,
distinctive in character;
but a magnetized
mirror of the other;

You are my alter ego;
it's as if you've always
been with me;
I can't imagine being
without you – always

Foxes

He opened his heart to me,
never sensing I'd make him cry,
just spread his arms wide,
didn't see the deceit in my eye;

If he hadn't been so naive,
really innocent like a child,
perhaps he would have discerned
duplicity lurking all the while;

It's not that I meant to hurt him,
never fanned the wildfires burning,
but, they always glowed within me
and kept the sinister yearning;

I've hurt so many along the way,
but, most of them just got mad,
except this man was different,
his beautiful eyes became sad;

I knew I'd messed up big time,
and I wanted to take it all back,
wanted to beg his sweet forgiveness
and promise to pick up the slack;

But foxes can't change colors,
no sense in me telling a lie,
the back door's always calling
and I knew I'd tip on the sly;

So, I lost another good one,
watched him turn with sigh,
but, I couldn't muster the decency
to say I'm sorry or goodbye

If

if you were to stand
too close to me,
my breath would
be taken away
on wings of
expectancy; I'd
have no energy
left for a whisper
to the lilting breeze;

should you gently take
my hand, and
caress it in yours,
my heart would
stop, and seal that
precious second
for all eternity;

if ever you dared
to brush my lips
with the sweetness
of yours, my head
would swoon, my
senses would defy
me, and I'd faint
from a pleasure
too exquisite to
endure

Come Midnight

I love a man
    I don't yet know;

  He's a stranger
    who's captured
my heart,
  captivated
my thoughts and
    concealed my
future happiness
  in his;

This man's a distant
  longing, pulling
within my soul,
    a Herculean tugging,
just beyond my
      touch;

A faceless intruder,
  marking time,
    at the watchman's
bidding,

  But, come
midnight, as sleep
carries me out to sea,
  I whisper
his name

A Mother's Prayer
(In the Name of Him)

Thank you, Father, for you've trusted me,
and given me an awesome responsibility;
knowing better than I, what I'm a capable of,
you sent the Holy Spirit to guide my love,

over two little ones, so precious and dear,
they're a blessing to have and a joy to be near;
Like a lyric of love that sings my smile,
they make hours of motherhood worth the while;

It's through your grace, I have maternal logic,
to discern whatever problems they may get;
Each day, I kiss their hurts and I dry their tears;
With your mercy, I'll be there throughout their years;

You've taught me to share with them abundantly,
the teachings of what you want them to be;
I humbly accept the precious gift of these two,
and promise to love and protect in the name of you.

This Day

Envelope me in your arms,
     this night,
       just as I've held you captive
in my thoughts
     this day;

Surround me with sounds,
   playfully sensual,
     to encase the
fervent musings that
    have plagued me
     all day;

Embrace me passionately,
   with your eyes, your
   hands, and let your
lips compose lyrics
    across the canvas
     of my body;

Extinguish the flames,
    this night,
   that threaten to sear
    with a heat of a
spurious sun.

Farewell Note

I'm moving on.

Leaving behind
   a river of tears;

It can't get no worse,
   couldn't possibly
hurt no deeper;

Don't like feeling
   like a fool,
being accused,
   being used;

Somewhere
   in time, maybe
on those solitary
nights,
I disappeared;

Morphed by your
   insecurities,
swallowed by
   my suspicions,
I no longer knew
     myself;

So, I'm moving on...

Gonna let this rush
   of tears be my
farewell note, a

mighty, thunderous
   crest left crashing
in my wake.

Printed in the United States
By Bookmasters